MRS MERTON'S
FRIENDSHIP BOOK

Mrs Merton was born in the middle of the 1930s
Depression, in the same two-up, two-down terraced house
in Heaton Norris, Stockport, in which she lives today with
her husband, Mr Merton, and her 35-year-old son Malcolm.

Following a spell as a radio Agony Aunt, her warm
personality and ready wit soon caught the attention of TV
moguls in the north-west area. Within months, she'd gone
national all over the country with her celebrity chat show,
The Mrs Merton Show, which begins its third series in
autumn 1996.

MRS MERTON'S FRIENDSHIP BOOK

Something here for you to think about for each day of the year

Caroline Hook
Craig Cash and
Henry Normal

FOURTH ESTATE • *London*

This paperback edition first published 1996
First published in Great Britain in 1995 by
Fourth Estate Limited
6 Salem Road
London W2 4BU

A catalogue record for this book is available from the
British Library.

ISBN 1–85702–548–2

Typeset by Palimpsest Book Production Limited,
Polmont, Stirlingshire
Printed in Great Britain by the Bath Press Ltd,
Bath, Bath

Acknowledgements

We would like to acknowledge the timely interjections of Peter Hook, the catering skills of Maureen Aherne, the doghandling capabilities of Renee Gillis, the magic fingers of Angela Pell, the patience of Stephanie Davies, the accommodating nature of Jean and Jim Cash, the vivacious exuberance of Jan Murphy, the palate of Carol Gally, the exposure of Matt Squire, the maternal guidance of Sally Holloway, the cherubic face of David Gorman, the schoolboy charm of Andy Harries and the absence of Peter Kessler.

And for help with photographs, the following: Nigel Joynson and staff, Fletcher Moss Botanical Gardens, the ladies at Fletcher Moss café, Suttons Seeds, Dr and Mrs Tobias, Brookside Garden Centre, Poynton, the *Telegraph* Colour Library for the kittens on the book jacket, and Sylvia Saunders, Paula, Gail and Melanie at Saunders Hair Studio, Hazel Grove.

'For a friend of mine, Lily'

January

January 1st, Monday, New Year's Day

HAPPY New Year!

January 2nd, Tuesday

A VERY elderly aunt of mine Florrie Anderson, occasionally comes to visit me. She is in her 90s – a white-haired frail old lady who is still fully compos mentis at the time of writing. Sadly she is stricken with acute incontinence through no fault of her own. Whenever she visits, Mr Merton's nerves are on edge the whole time. Although he refuses to be in the same room, he does tend to hover in the hallway with a scrubbing brush and bucket. I'm sure Florrie realises this and it only adds to her distress. Mr Merton would prefer me to visit her, but it's too far away and I would have to catch two buses. Sometimes men are quite insensitive.

January 3rd, Wednesday

How on earth did Gandhi manage to walk so far in flip-flops? I can't last ten minutes in mine.

January 4th, Thursday

T IM Rice and Andrew Lloyd Webber live in a fantasy world. They seem to be under the impression that everybody bursts into song at the drop of a hat. Eva Perón would surely not have been singing during her Argentinian crisis years and certainly not in the West End.

January 5th, Friday
Children are a Blessing!
THERE'S no greater delight than holding a newborn baby in your arms. This truly is God's greatest work! What a pity their heads are so wobbly.

January 6th, Saturday
IT'S so important these days to be politically aware, especially in the North West. Every month, myself, my friend Lily and six other women friends get together and discuss and debate current political issues of the day and 'put the world to rights', over tea and a light snack. We have solved most of the country's major issues in this simple but effective fashion. If ever the conversation is in danger of becoming bogged down in political rhetoric, Connie Bywaters takes the opportunity of blacking up, donning a wig and regaling us all with her Tina Turner rendition of 'What's Love Got to Do with It?' If only they'd emulate this in the House of Commons, more people would take an interest in political debate and the country wouldn't be in such a mess.

Housebound, not me!

January 7th, Sunday

*M*R *Merton is a huge fan of David Hasselhoff.* He has seen everything he has been in recently, with the exception of 'Knightrider'.

January 8th, Monday

*O*NE *of my favourite pastimes is to accompany my friend Kate Sullivan, who spends her free time viewing the interior of houses that are for sale.* She is very thorough, and will not leave without giving her opinion. What the estate agents and vendors do not realise is that Kate has no intention of purchasing any of these houses. On the contrary, she has a total balance of £7.50 in her current account and has lived in a council maisonette for 35 years. When challenged about her pretence, she explains that with the home-buying market in decline, her interest gives that little bit of hope to the vendors. Well done Kate! She's managed to combine her natural curiosity with a public service!

January 9th, Tuesday
Take This Take That

*T*AKE *That are here to stay.* Their natural talents have won through. Not since Cliff Richards sang 'Power to All Our Friends' on the Eurovision Song Contest have we seen such coordinated clever footwork and dance capabilities.

January 10th, Wednesday

LET'S hear it for Kiwi Fruit! It's like a tropical banana with added interest.

January 11th, Thursday

*D*ELIA *Smith made millions out of what can only be described as cooking.* We all do it but most of us don't expect to be paid vast amounts.

January 12th, Friday

'*K*ISS *it better Mummy'* is the cry when your child has grazed his knee or banged his little head. With my son, Malcolm, the kiss on the sore spot from me would immediately stop his crying and wailing. However, as every mother must face, there comes a time when you have to give way to modern medicine,

and a kiss from Mummy is no match for keyhole
surgery and the like.

January 13th, Saturday

*F*OR *years the BBC has done a programme called
'Desert Island Discs' where people choose their eight*
favourite records to take with them on a desert island.
Surely the most important things would be food and
medical supplies. These people live in cloud cuckoo land.

January 14th, Sunday

*O*N *this day Lily's mother Rose will be 100 years
old, and is looking forward to receiving a telegram
from the Queen.* It seems a scant reward for what is,
after all, a century. Come on Queen Elizabeth, give us
some incentive!

January 15th, Monday

*C*HUCK *Berry penned the words 'My Ding-a-Ling, My
Ding-a-Ling, I want you to play with My Ding-a-
Ling'.* If only he'd given a thought to how these lyrics
could be misconstrued by lewd-minded folk.

January 16th, Tuesday

*S*CHOOL *days are the happiest days of your life!*
Not so for my son Malcolm though, sadly. He
never seemed to make any friends at school, despite
being immaculately turned out in his uniform and

cap. However, he did form a strong relationship with his class gerbil – and spent his dinner-hours regaling 'Browny' (the gerbil) with tales of his imaginary friends.

January 17th, Wednesday

*I*T'S *always a worry when going on holiday that you're leaving your house empty and prone to being burglarised.* A little tip I picked up from travel-wise Judith Chalmers is to place a mop by the window with one of your coats on – burglars will think you are in and will, with a bit of luck, burgle next door.

January 18th, Thursday

*S*ALVADOR *Dali – daft as a brush.*

January 19th, Friday

*L*AUGHTER *is the best medicine.* Why not do yourself the world of good – have a laugh today. If you can't find anything to laugh at, visit a friend with a funny face.

January 20th, Saturday

*M*Y *friend Sarah Pell has a lovely daughter Angela who has just become a glamorous air hostess for British Airways.* It is a marvellous job, which involves flying all around the world serving busy businessmen with drinks and little prepacked dinners. What a far cry from her previous job, helping out in a local café. Well done Angela! You're a credit to your mother (who never shuts up about you).

January 21st, Sunday

Has anyone ever noticed how Helen Keller, the popular deaf, blind, and dumb girl sounds very like Henry Kelly the popular presenter of 'Going For Gold'?

January 22nd, Monday

The sixties are well documented as a time of liberation and hedonism. Not so for my friend Rita Clegg, who suffered an excessive wind disorder throughout this decade. What with the Sixties revival now in full swing, poor Rita lives in constant fear of a relapse.

January 23rd, Tuesday

Don't be Too Quick to Judge!

At number 47 a lady on her own moved in. Over the period of the first few weeks my friend Lily and I watched a parade of male visitors, each of which stopped for about an hour and then left. It was only after we presented the Mayor with a 100-name petition from local residents to have this prostitute ousted that we discovered she was in fact a piano teacher.

January 24th, Wednesday

Breast implants are not for the faint-hearted!

January 25th, Thursday

*F*OR *many years I have corresponded with a penpal called Jessica Kessler who lives in Ontario, Canada.* It has been a great source of pleasure to me, exchanging news and views from our different backgrounds. However, one morning my initial delight at receiving one of her distinctive airmail letters turned to despair – she had written telling me of her impending visit to England, where she wished to call in on my country mansion. I found myself regretting a few exaggerations I had included in my letters. I was left with no alternative but to write back and inform her that due to Lord Merton's tropical disease picked up on safari, we could not possibly accommodate her this season in Heaton Norris. I know on this particular occasion I may have stretched the truth a little, but it is important for us to give a good impression of England to these foreign folk.

January 26th, Friday

*T*ODAY *is Australia Day when all round the world people are celebrating Australia.* Why it's got the nickname 'down under', I'll never know.

January 27th, Saturday

A FRIEND *of mine Tilly Morgan woke up one morning believing herself to have started 'The Change'.* After ringing round her friends to tell of her hot flush, she discovered her husband Brian had inadvertently left the central heating on high all night and it was a false alarm. I must have said to Tilly a thousand times – Nature will not be rushed!

January 28th, Sunday

*L*INDA *McCartney is a barmpot!* Not content with living a luxurious life as wife of one of the richest men in Britain, she's come up with a crazy scheme to make burgers with no meat in them.

January 29th, Monday

*S*OME *time ago my friend Irene Jacobson caused quite a stir in the local community by being seen in public sporting a pair of leggings.* She should never forget that what looks good on an 18-year-old fashion model in the catalogue is not necessarily right for a 66-year-old bookie's clerk from Chorley with elephantitus in her left knee. Let this be a lesson to us all.

January 30th, Tuesday

*A*s *a young boy my son Malcolm always wanted to become a fireman extinguishing deadly fires and saving lives.* His ambitions lasted until he left school when he was forced to face up to the fact that the hazardous role of fireman was not suited to his weak disposition and delicate tummy. He now works in the local library, providing a service just as necessary for the community as fire-fighting.

January 31st, Wednesday

*D*ON'T *dismay!* An ending is always sadder than a beginning! Don't think of today as the end of January, think of it as the day before the beginning of February. That's the ticket!

February

February 1st, Thursday
THE Death Penalty – is it enough?

February 2nd, Friday
*M*R *Merton has that enviable quality of being able to nod off at any time of the day.* Many's the time I'll be giving him the benefit of my advice only to turn around and find him fast asleep like a baby with a string of saliva dangling from the side of his mouth. Does his vacant expression betray dreams of fame and fortune, of ambitions never realised, aspirations never fulfilled, or is it that same one involving Gina Lollobrigida and a young pony? We shall never really know for certain.

February 3rd, Saturday
I NEVER *understood the feminist back-lash against Benny Hill.* There were always plenty of women in his programme and they were always good-looking.

February 4th, Sunday
S PARE *a thought for my friend Eliza Hamilton, who was wrongly diagnosed as mentally unstable when all she was was a bit giddy.*

February 5th, Monday

*A*LFRED *Hitchcock's films are always spine-chilling psychological thrillers with a sinister twist.* However, he thoughtfully always included himself in a rib-tickling cameo appearance – complete with his funny little face and portly stature, as if to reassure us it was all only make-believe after all.

February 6th, Tuesday

CHILDREN *say the funniest things!* Unfortunately I can't remember any of them.

February 7th, Wednesday

*A*FRIEND *of mine Maureen Regan always pronounces the D in Wednesday – the first D, that is.* I've challenged her on this point several times but she refuses to discuss it logically and we end up at loggerheads.

February 8th, Thursday

THERE'S nothing worse than being egg-bound. It happens to us all at some stage in our lives but for poor Mr Merton this is a recurring ailment. We've tried everything to alleviate this problem, from a bag of prunes to acupuncture. I've heard of a cure in the USA, but Mr Merton refuses to let me start up a nationwide appeal on his behalf to raise the money. He even gets upset if I mention it outside our immediate family. Thus he remains a martyr to his bowels.

February 9th, Friday

LET'S hear it for Penelope Keith! Such a consummate professional. An all-round character actress who can portray a posh lady in any environment.

February 10th, Saturday

PARENTS should take an interest in their children's education. I always made a point of attending each parents' evening when Malcolm was at school. The problem I had was that, with Malcolm not having the most domineering of personalities, I'd have to produce a recent photo of him as the teachers had forgotten who he was.

February 11th, Sunday

*E*VERYONE *loves to cry at weddings.* Are we crying because the bride looks so radiant and pure, and the groom looks so proud and strong? Or are we crying at the remembrance of our own catastrophic attempt at matrimony? No matter how much you tell people, they must make their own mistakes.

February 12th, Monday

Abraham Lincoln's Birthday
No need to send a card, he's dead at the moment.
Happy Birthday anyway Mr Lincoln.

February 13th, Tuesday

*N*ICK *Owen is a real tonic.* Any time I see his cheeky face on TV it brightens my day. Mr Merton, on the other hand, says he can't stomach his continuous smirking gormless flannel. Nick Owen is the only celebrity Mr Merton and I disagree about. Perhaps the Nick Owen phenomena needs to be investigated at a higher level and sorted out once and for all.

February 14th, Wednesday, Valentine's Day

Guess Who?
> *A Valentine's card comes in the door*
> *With special greetings from your amour.*
> *Is the sender an Arabic sheikh*
> *Or a bald-headed pensioner, mild and meek?*
> *Well, for myself I fear the latter:*
> *It's from Mr Merton, he's mad as a hatter!*

Why not pamper yourself!

A very special Valentine's Day to my one and only sweetheart, Mr Merton, the daft old goat.

February 15th, Thursday
ALL this talk about Glasnost and Perestroika! Who even knows where they are?

February 16th, Friday
IT'S all very well nowadays with the likes of Australians such as Jason and Kylie taking their popularity for granted. Never forget it was Rolf Harris who came over here first and paved the way.

February 17th, Saturday
WHAT on earth was Adolf Hitler thinking of?

February 18th, Sunday
WHAT a topsy-turvy world night workers must suffer from. They get up when we go to bed, they go to bed when we get up. Our breakfast-time is their tea-time. Goodness, what a 'to-do'!

February 19th, Monday
WE were delighted to hear Mr Merton's only sister Anne Merton was to be getting married. For too long she had been known as the spinster of the parish and had decided to do something about it with a gentleman from Switzerland who was very big in the chocolate world. For months we heard of how she

was going to marry him and live in a log cabin in the
Alps – indeed we were a tad tired of her boasting!
This fairy-tale romance turned sour on the eve of her
wedding night when she received a note pushed through
the door saying her husband-to-be felt he could not go
through with the marriage as they came from different
backgrounds which could not merge. He knew how hurt
she'd be so he enclosed, as a token, two quarter-pound
bars of plain chocolate. Poor jilted Anne could not bring
herself to eat this fine Swiss chocolate but fortunately
she had caring friends in myself and my friend Lily, who
had the presence of mind to polish it off sharpish.

February 20th, Tuesday

*E*RIC *Morley from Miss World was so versatile.*
Anybody could read out the winners' names in the
traditional way but he mastered the art of reading them
in reverse order.

February 21st, Wednesday

*O*NE *morning I was awoken by a gentle prodding in
the small of my back.* After my initial terror had
subsided I realised Mr Merton had unpicked the lock
on my bedroom door after having another one of his
'Gina Lollobrigida' dreams, and crawled in bed with
me with only one thought on his mind. Reticent in that
department at the best of times, I thought quickly for
a diversion. I told him he would be much more enticing
to me equipped with his set of dentures. So he dashed

off to his boxroom to prepare himself. Yes readers, you've guessed it, quick as a flash I locked the door behind him and refused him entry until his ardour had subsided. If only Miss Lollobrigida knew the trouble she causes in the North West area.

February 22nd, Thursday
SACHA Distel and Julio Iglesias are much of a muchness – but thankfully there's room for both.

February 23rd, Friday
SARAH Miles is renowned for drinking her own urine every morning for health reasons. I prefer fresh orange juice, and so does my friend Lily.

February 24th, Saturday
I LOVE to hear a heart-warming story about a good Samaritan, but I can't understand all the fuss. I've never met a bad Samaritan.

February 25th, Sunday
NEVER judge a book by its cover! Never has this been more apparent than in the tragic case of Maud Carols (spinster). Although grotesque in the facial department, she is kind to a fault with a sunny disposition. How sad people never get to see these qualities as they are all too quick to point out her imperfections – big jug ears, protruding forehead and huge brown buck teeth.

February 26th, Monday
Too many undeserving people are receiving OBEs and Knighthoods from the Queen. She seems to be giving them away willy-nilly these days, trying to curry favour. These awards should be restricted to worthy individuals. Desmond Lynam springs to mind here.

February 27th, Tuesday, Pancake Day
WHY not have a pancake?

February 28th, Wednesday
AMERICAN elections always seem so much more fun than ours. They have streamers, balloons and ticker-tape. Maybe the British Government should follow their lead and not take it all so seriously.

March

March 1st, Friday

SYLVIA McCoid was for years the local midwife and revered as the soul of discretion. However, due to National Health cutbacks and an upsetting burglary involving her electrical equipment, she snapped under the pressure one Bank Holiday Monday. She is now seen in the town centre in overcoat and slippers shouting personal details of local women's anatomy to anyone who'll listen.

March 2nd, Saturday

WHO does Jeremy Paxman think he's kidding? Someone should tell him he's not Bamber Gascoigne. Nothing would induce me to think he is.

March 3rd, Sunday

YOU can't beat a luxury caravan holiday. You really are your own boss. Unlike Bed and Breakfast, you can come and go as you please. No one tells you what to do. It's a holiday for the more adventurous amongst us.

March 4th, Monday

*S*IGMUND *Freud was a very lewd man*. His fans try to pass him off as intellectual but as far as I'm concerned he had a one-track mind and a sewer mentality. He was the Roy 'Chubby' Brown of his day, but never as funny.

March 5th, Tuesday

*W*HAT *with the worry of the mortgage and bills etc. men often forget to wash their personal bits and pieces as often as they should, and sweat does accumulate, no matter where you live.* A friend of mine, Bridie Caldwell, found that embroidering the name of her husband's favourite football team on to his flannel made him more inclined to use it on a regular basis. Nice one Bridie!

March 6th, Wednesday

*W*ILLY *Rushton never did it for me – I could never see the sense of him.*

March 7th, Thursday

*T*HIS *day last year my son Malcolm was at an all-time low. He was an invalid by way of an ingrown toenail.* I can still picture him now, his foot propped up on a stool, watching 'Countdown' and bravely trying to smile through the pain at one of Richard Whiteley's hilarious puns.

March 8th, Friday

*T*HINGS *were a lot more innocent in the old days.*
If two women were dancing together in public you
would just assume they were both widowed and think
nothing untoward.

March 9th, Saturday

*W*HY *has David Jensen dropped the 'Kid' from his
name – you knew where you were with him then.*

March 10th, Sunday

*H*ow *can people complain about the length of time
spent waiting in Outpatients for an appointment?* I've
spent many happy hours in our local hospital familiarising
myself with people's ailments and afflictions.

March 11th, Monday

*W*HATEVER *happened to the 'Black and White Minstrel Show'?* It truly was a ground-breaking series. You never saw black people on television before this. It was ahead of its time.

March 12th, Tuesday
Under the Doctor

A FRIEND *of mine Joyce Muir (née Appleton) has been a doctor's receptionist longer than she cares to remember.* She's worked there that long now she can diagnose patient illness over the phone, thus saving the doctor home visits. She gets it wrong occasionally, but what can you expect, she's not had the 7 years' intensive training he has. At least she has a go!

March 13th, Wednesday, Commonwealth Day

*H*APPY *Commonwealth Day.*

March 14th, Thursday

A WELL-KNOWN *local simpleton friend of mine Percy Pendleton has the unique ability to name different species of fish just by sight alone.* It is locally regarded that there is no fish known to man that Percy cannot name. If only he could turn this ability to his advantage, the sky would be the limit for Percy.

March 15th, Friday

ENOUGH talk of Maastricht. Why doesn't the Government bring back Green Shield Stamps?

March 16th, Saturday

ORANGES are Not the Only Fruit' was the name of a popular TV show. How right they were. Look at lemons and limes!

March 17th, Sunday, St Patrick's Day

LET'S hear it for the Patron Saint of Ireland. We're well into the nineties yet he's still one of the most popular and famous saints in the British Isles.

March 18th, Monday

I REMEMBER when continental quilts were first invented in our high-street shops. They were considered very cosmopolitan. Nowadays no one gives them a second thought. Proof if proof were needed. Progress is not always as obvious as you might think.

March 19th, Tuesday

THE Eurovision Song Contest is a great way to unite different countries across Europe. What a shame it is usually a very dismal affair with lots of foreigners singing songs none of us can make head nor tail of. This does not bode well for Maastricht.

Someone's bound to know!

March 20th, Wednesday

WHEN will people start forgetting that Desmond Lynam dated a transvestite?

March 21st, Thursday

WHY are women never game-show hosts? Come on Germaine Greer, you can show these men a thing or two. You can give Henry Kelly a run for his money.

March 22nd, Friday

LENA Zavaroni – what a belter!

March 23rd, Saturday

THERE are two men in my life – one of them I have tried to teach right from wrong, good from bad, and how to survive the adult world. To the other one I have been a mother. To Mr Merton and Malcolm, thank you for being you, warts and all.

March 24th, Sunday

I RECEIVED a poem off Malcolm my son one Mother's Day:

> *Thank you mother for being so kind*
> *I often think of you in my mind*
> *You're always so kind and loving*
> *I never think of you as nothing.*

I could barely read it through the tears streaming down my face. He knows how important a mother's love is. I think that's why he has never left home.

March 25th, Monday

THANK goodness for clever boffins! Where would we be without them!

March 26th, Tuesday

WHAT a shame a promising musical career never developed for that inbred banjo-picking young boy in the film 'Deliverance' starring Burt Reynolds.

March 27th, Wednesday

LONG may Lesley Joseph continue to entertain us with her comedy caricatures and funny face. Let's make the most of her before Hollywood beckons.

March 28th, Thursday

WHAT are the hyenas laughing at?

March 29th, Friday

ON a day trip to Knowsley Safari Park (just outside Liverpool) Mr Merton and myself marvelled at the uncomplicated lifestyles of animals in the wild. How sophisticated we must seem to them in our Morris Minor.

March 30th, Saturday

IN the library where my son Malcolm works he became convinced that people were taking out large-print books who didn't really need them. He became withdrawn and worried, sick about the injustice of it all.

Sometimes I wish Malcolm didn't work in such a volatile environment.

March 31st, Sunday, British Summer Time Begins

WELL *done to everyone concerned.* British Summer Time is always bang on. They certainly know their business.

April

April 1st, Monday, April Fools' Day!

I ONCE *played a trick on a friend of mine, Lily.* She rang me one morning and I told her I couldn't stay talking on the telephone as I had two pork chops under the grill. You've probably guessed already. Yes, this was a trick as they were, in fact, lamb chops! Poor Lily fell for that one hook, line and sinker! She hadn't realised the date was the first of April so naturally she was unprepared.

I did, of course, ring her back after twelve o'clock to tell her and luckily she saw the funny side. We still laugh about it to this very day. I only have to say 'pork chops' and Lily bursts into spontaneous giggles.

Why not try this trick yourself. Bear in mind, it doesn't necessarily have to be chops for those on a budget.

April 2nd, Tuesday
My Birthday

I WAS *a little worried about putting my birthday in as I was afraid I would be inundated with cards and expensive gifts from well-wishers.* This is a chance I'll have to take.

April 3rd, Wednesday

Roy's the Boy!
HATS off to Roy Walker! He's made presenting
'Catchphrase' his own.

April 4th, Thursday

*M*ONEY *doesn't buy happiness!* An acquaintance of
mine who shall remain nameless save for her
surname Doodsen inherited a large sum of money from
an unknown Australian benefactor. However, Elsie's
delight was short-lived as, on her way back from the
reading of the will, she lost her contact lens in the
Woodhouse Rd. As she stooped blindly to retrieve the
lens she was severely killed by the rush-hour traffic. All
the money in the world couldn't have saved her. Now
God has an angel with one contact lens! Something
there for us all to think about.

April 5th, Friday, Good Friday

*HALIBUT, mackerel, flounder, plaice – let's hear it for all
fish, not just cod!*

April 6th, Saturday

*N*EIL *Armstrong – not the hero we thought he was!*
Yes we were all jubilant at his trip to the moon,
but what has he done since? It is people who are
constantly campaigning and pushing the barriers who
get my vote, like Esther Rantzen.

The sporting life!

April 7th, Sunday, Easter Sunday
Easter Lament

I LAMENT the demise of the Easter Bonnet at this time of year. For some women in a loveless marriage it was their only chance of happiness, now sadly taken away from them by an uncaring modern society. For pity's sake why not bring back the bonnet!

April 8th, Monday, Easter Monday

T HERE is some confusion as to why we give and receive eggs at Easter. Let's clear this matter up once and for all. A friend of mine Lily says Jesus himself was partial to eggs (free range), indeed all dairy products. However, this is pure bunkum! In fact none of Lily's historical explanations bear up under close inspection.

The truth of the matter is the egg symbolises the rock moved away from Jesus's tomb. However, chocolate manufacturers have been quick to cash in on this biblical escapade. Playing on children's gullibility, they have even inserted Smarties which we all know could not have been around in Jesus's day.

April 9th, Tuesday

WHY not make a new friend today? Friends are like jewels – keep rubbing them and they'll remain shiny.

April 10th, Wednesday

SPRING HARVEST
Daisy brings her daisies
Rose brings her roses
Heather brings her heather
And Lily there, empty-handed and vacant.

April 11th, Thursday
Is there anywhere Judith Chalmers hasn't been?

April 12th, Friday
*A*LEARNED *friend of mine Henry House once told me of his lifelong ambition to pilot a passenger-carrying plane of the Boeing 707 Series.* However, his

numerous requests to aviation authorities have been refused as he has no previous experience.

April 13th, Saturday

GOD bless Shane Richie.

April 14th, Sunday

*M*y friend Patricia (I call her Pat – we all do) *proudly showed me her new security light she's had fitted recently in her back garden.* She explained the light comes on when burglars set foot anywhere near her doorway. However, whilst talking, I stepped out on to the patio and to my astonishment the light came on. As you can imagine I was distraught, I have never stolen anything in my life! Modern gadgets are all very well but they're not to be trusted over common decent folk.

April 15th, Monday

IT'S a small world! Especially for my friend Peggy Asher who is housebound!

April 16th, Tuesday

IT is a pity Shakespeare isn't alive today. How he'd rejoice in actresses such as Dame Judi Dench, and the American Whoopi Goldberg.

April 17th, Wednesday

WHILST travelling in the back of a taxi to visit my old school friend Winnie (known locally for her warm personality and spectacular handwriting skills), I couldn't help noticing that the taxi man was completely bald, headwise.

Nevertheless, not to be outdone, on to the back of his shiny bald head he had thoughtfully tatooed a smile! Full marks for initiative! Something there for other bald taxi drivers to think about.

April 18th, Thursday

CALLING all youngsters in need of a role model! Look no further than Desmond Lynam, the popular sports commentator and personality.

April 19th, Friday

A FRIEND of mine Lily gave me this poem she'd written herself.

> **SPRING'S THE THING!**
> *Spring's the thing!*
> *The sleight of the hand,*
> *An old curtain ring*
> *Come Martians land.*

They have since changed her medication.

April 20th, Saturday

SPARE a thought for Rula Lenska and Dennis Waterman.

April 21st, Sunday, the Queen's Birthday

I WAS delighted last year when the great Cliff Richards got knighted. However, my delight was short-lived as it took me an entire afternoon to go through my record collection prefixing his name with Sir. I wonder if the Queen knew what trouble she was causing at the time?

April 22nd, Monday

EXACTLY 15 years today since my hysterectomy, but I don't like to dwell.

April 23rd, Tuesday, St George's Day

I ALWAYS remember a friend of Mr Merton's called George Parry on this day. He is one of those stalwarts of society – a night security man for a local casual-wear factory. Night after night, he alone guards the empty building, with only a television and thermos for comfort. He is one of the many unsung heroes called George to be remembered on this day. Good on you George!

April 24th, Wednesday

FOND memories I have of Aled Jones.

April 25th, Thursday
Let Sleeping Dogs Lie!

*M*Y *friend Peggy unearthed a huge Welsh dresser which she believed to date back to King Richard the Lionheart.* Hearing that the 'Antiques Roadshow' was coming to the next village she immediately hired a transit van to carry her valuable find the necessary ten miles. Needless to say she was exhilarated at the prospect of seeking a precise evaluation and the chance to appear in front of millions of viewers. However, Hugh Scully unkindly proclaimed it worthless, and after the show even refused to go halves with the now devastated Peggy on the cost of the transit van. This is the side of the 'Antiques Roadshow' we seldom see!

April 26th, Friday

*T*RAMS *are not buses and yet they're not trains.* They are somewhere in between. A different form of transport altogether! Whatever next I wonder?

April 27th, Saturday

A GOOD *marriage is like a bourbon biscuit – two crispy chocolate-flavoured biscuits sandwiched together by a rich creamy brown filling. Just like marriage!*

April 28th, Sunday

*S*INCE *the privatisation of electricity both myself and Eileen Bolton have found no increase in the quality* *of electricity.* If anything, 40-watt bulbs seem duller on my landing. Are we being short-changed?

April 29th, Monday

*D*ON'T *be intimidated by the fancy name Vol-au-vents.* Eric and June Selby from Chorley, Lancs avoided Vol-au-vents for over 20 years, ignorant of the fact they are merely pastry with a simple filling. This is a common mistake amongst working-class folk. Such a shame!

April 30th, Tuesday

70 YEARS YOUNG!

Look in the mirror it's your birthday
Your whole head has now turned grey
You're older now and a lot more wise
See the crows' feet around your eyes
Smile a little, that's the deal,
Although your teeth may not be real
Keep morbid thoughts of death at bay
Be cheery it's your special day!

May

May 1st, Wednesday, May Day

*M*AY *Day!* This is the only day of the year that shares its name with an international rescue signal! Don't miss out on all the fun.

May 2nd, Thursday
Why Not Stay In and Diet?
Plan a diet for a day:

Breakfast – an apple
Lunch – an apple
Tea – an apple

I call that the 'apple' diet.

May 3rd, Friday

*T*HERE'S *always something to be thankful for!* If you've got arthritis in your left arm – rejoice in your right arm (and vice versa, if it's the other way round). If you've not got arthritis at all you can still rejoice. Other possibilities – psoriasis, lock jaw and eczema.

May 4th, Saturday

A FRIEND *of mine June from Harper Hay lives next to a Satanist.* What with all the carrying on she's not been able to enjoy a single episode of 'Cracker'.

43

May 5th, Sunday

Who thought of inventing the wheel? Full marks to that man!

May 6th, Monday

Synchronised swimming is not for the faint-hearted! It requires hours of practice. It is now an Olympic event and should not be confused with messing about in the water with 5 friends.

May 7th, Tuesday

When stopped by a passing motorist asking directions, if you haven't a clue of the way, be definite as you make it up. The important thing is to sound convincing.

May 8th, Wednesday

The Ten Commandments, here's a little tip. If you can't remember them, put a little sticker on your fridge door.

May 9th, Thursday

The computer will never take the place of the human brain. Can a computer rub calamine lotion on a sunburnt child's shoulders? I think not! Can a computer tell you your shampoo and set looks a million dollars? I think not! Can a computer surprise you with a weekend trip to a little guest-house 3 miles outside Southport? I think not! No – computers are one thing, but the human brain is another thing entirely. Think on!

Malcolm playing up!

May 10th, Friday

*C*OMEDIANS *Ahoy!* Take a leaf out of Ken Dodd's book. He's never had to resort to blue material to get a laugh. Take heed Ben Elton and Co.! The sooner this fad is out of your system the better.

May 11th, Saturday

Love Will Find a Way!

A VISUALLY *impaired friend of mine, whose husband incidentally has a cleft palate, recently celebrated her ruby wedding anniversary – 50 years of marriage despite each other's imperfections. How they met, however, is another story.*

May 12th, Sunday

*C*HALK *and cheese – Joanna Lumley and Boris Becker.*

May 13th, Monday

I'VE *got a little teaser for you, Mr Merton's party piece:*

> *What's long and thin*
> *covered in skin*
> *red in parts*
> *and goes in tarts?*

Answer – Rhubarb.

May 14th, Tuesday

*M*ANY *people think it's not 'with-it' to be Christian.* That it's for safe, comfortable, middle-of-the-road types. Nothing could be further from the truth, look at Cliff Richards with his Christmas number ones and his speciality dancing.

May 15th, Wednesday

Face Your Fears!

A CLOSE *relative of Mr Merton (his only sister, Anne) was plagued throughout her early life with an irrational fear of Ancient Egyptian mummies.* To conquer this phobia she decided to face it head-on and flew the 3,000 miles to Egypt where she forced herself to venture into the inner sanctum of Tutankhamun's tomb. She returned home in debt to the tune of over £2,000 for travel and accommodation but found her journey had not been in vain. She can now walk the streets of West Gorton and Stalybridge without fear of Ancient Egyptian mummies and their like. Money well spent.

May 16th, Thursday

*S*PARE *a thought for identical twins.* They may look pleasing on the eye but it's not always the fun we imagine it to be.

May 17th, Friday

A COUPLE *I know the Drapers (Mr and Mrs Draper) tried for years to have a baby by natural methods, but to no avail.* Their need for a child was so strong they eventually decided after much discussion to seek adoption. However, this poor childless Draper couple were refused on the grounds that they were both in their mid-sixties. They have now got a Jack Russell called Timothy (Timothy Draper).

May 18th, Saturday

I PERSONALLY *never eat muesli despite the extensive advertisement campaigns.* No amount of sweet talk can persuade me otherwise. The more they try, the more I dig my heels in. That's one in the eye for advertisers and their ilk!

May 19th, Sunday, Islamic New Year

A HAPPY New Year to all my Islamic readers.

May 20th, Monday

*S*ID *Little has been the butt of Eddie Large for many years.* We all assume it never bothers him. Only he knows the truth.

May 21st, Tuesday

*S*TOCKPORT *is well worth a visit!* There are shops and other amenities and it has easy access by bus or train. Why not make a day of it? (Remember – avoid Sunday if it's the shops you want.)

May 22nd, Wednesday

Beware the Green-Eyed Monster (Jealousy)!

*A*s *a young girl I was always jealous of my friend Dora Burrows.* When we did a school project Dora got top marks and I was jealous. When we did the Whit walks Dora had the best dress and I was jealous. When we went to the dancehalls Dora would always be asked to dance by handsome chaps and I was jealous. As time progressed I lost touch with Dora. A few years ago I heard she'd been in a terrible accident and was paralysed from the neck down and a funny thing happened – I was no longer jealous of her. Tragic as this seems, it's worth remembering every cloud has a silver lining.

May 23rd, Thursday

No one has yet invented a quick and easy way to clean stair carpets. Yet we've put a man on the moon. Come on all you inventor types, get cracking!

May 24th, Friday

Bring back 'Albion Market'!

May 25th, Saturday

Surprise, Surprise, it's Cilla's birthday! Thank you Cilla for all the many happy hours you've given the nation watching you on the box! Despite being a multimillionairess you've never lost that common touch! You are still, truly, our Cilla.

May 26th, Sunday

Don't shy away from disposable nappies. They give you the best of both worlds.

May 27th, Monday

One for the Ladies!

Mr Merton's oldest friend is a gentleman called Arthur Capstick. In his day he was a real Bobby dazzler and didn't we know it! He could charm the birds out of the trees and often did. Ladies would swoon at the mention of his name (Arthur Capstick). Even I was smitten at one time. Compared to Mr Merton he was always turned out a treat – always a shine on his shoes, a crease in his pants, never a hair out of place. The funny thing about Arthur is, despite all his appeal, he has never married and now lives on his own, save for the company of a 17-year-old Italian boy whom he has kindly taken under his wing.

May 28th, Tuesday

THE name Ken has been much abused since the onslaught of the Second World War! What has to be done before people will take this name seriously?

May 29th, Wednesday

MY self and a friend of mine Lily were shocked to hear of the sudden demise of Norma Walsh who lived by the local Dewhurst's. We immediately nipped round to pay our respects and secure a memory of her by obtaining some small trinket or other objet d'art of the deceased. On arriving there, out of breath, we were dismayed to find Mrs Stapleton and her sister were already leaving the house with arms full of Norma's clothes and sundries. Mr Walsh at least seemed comforted. He had no idea of Norma's popularity in the community. It's good to see the way folk rally round in a crisis.

May 30th, Thursday

BE mindful of other cultures! Whilst travelling in Turkey you will encounter ordinary men carrying small handbags. This is no cause for concern. It is a local custom and is in no way untoward.

May 31st, Friday
ROGER Moore is not Sean Connery and he never will be!

June

June 1st, Saturday

*P*OOR *Oscar Wilde!* He lived in the wrong time! Had he been alive today, his ready wit and repartee would surely have given Angus Deayton a run for his money.

June 2nd, Sunday

Starsigns – the Proof!

*A*STROLOGY *is not the complete codswollop most people think it is!* Your starsign and your health go hand in hand. There is undeniable proof that there is a direct link between your birthsign and your medical condition. Six of my friends who are Geminis have undergone hysterectomy operations. This cannot be coincidence! Something there for Geminis to look out for. Sagittarians on the cusp are prone to cystitis (the honeymoon disease).

June 3rd, Monday

*W*HAT *did the Russians think they were playing at – going Communist all those years. I bet there's a few red faces knocking around the Kremlin!*

June 4th, Tuesday

A *FRIEND* *of mine Lily and I were recently in a Chinese restaurant.* On the table to our left were an Indian family and on the table to our right two Italian students. We were all enjoying ourselves immensely at the hospitality of the Chinese. If only the UN could take our lead! Food is the international language and it always will be.

June 5th, Wednesday

I *HAD the pleasure to meet with Richard Madeley and Judy Finnigan – a nicer couple you couldn't meet.* I think it's great that no one ever mentions that Judy is the older one in this arrangement.

June 6th, Thursday

CALLING all lady drivers! Don't hang your handbag on the choke – it's not that sturdy, I know this from experience.

June 7th, Friday

SIR Isaac Newton has been lauded for too long! It doesn't take a genius to work out that if things fall they drop downwards. How Sir Isaac can claim to have invented it is beyond me and my friend Lily.

June 8th, Saturday

COME back Gilbert O'Sullivan. There's a gaping hole in the popular parade where you used to be.

June 9th, Sunday

I OFTEN look at Mr Merton and wonder what would have happened if I had married Richard Branson instead. No doubt the house would be decorated throughout. There's a man with get up and go!

June 10th, Monday

WHY not follow my lead? I like to have my son Malcolm's ears syringed on a regular basis.

June 11th, Tuesday

THE Brontë sisters were the Jilly Coopers of yesteryear, with their tales of romance and unrequited love. However, their novels sadly don't feature horses strongly, as do Jilly Cooper's.

June 12th, Wednesday

I ONLY speak one language (English) but never have a problem with any foreigners, who always seem to understand my facial grimaces and elaborate gestures.

June 13th, Thursday

You have to go a long way to top Barbara Cartland. She remains as youthful as ever. She's got it all!

June 14th, Friday

I REMEMBER the Queen being coronated as if it were yesterday. We had a wonderful street party with enough jelly for all. I can still remember the taste of the jelly on my tongue as if it was the first taste. I can only hope to be around when Prince Charles is coronated once again to taste that same jelly.

June 15th, Saturday

S CIENTISTS worldwide believe that the human being evolved from apes. This has never been more apparent than in the case of my friend Olive Stanton. A lovely woman who the local kids have no right calling 'Big Foot'.

June 16th, Sunday

I SN'T Sting an all-round good egg – pop singer, film actor and now he's saving the planet. What next!

June 17th, Monday

*M*R *Merton is getting on in years but he's still driving his Morris Minor.* I do worry as sometimes he's not very careful and forgets to indicate. When I challenge him on the subject he always replies, 'I've lived in the same road for 40 years and I think people know where I'm going by now.' It's a waste of time arguing with him when he's in one of these moods.

June 18th, Tuesday

*L*IONEL *Richie – never afraid to push back the barriers.*

June 19th, Wednesday

*S*TEVEN *Spielberg has developed the knack of knowing just what everyone is going to be talking about in six months' time.* He did it with a little ET and he did it again with Dinosaurs. It's no wonder his new films are always in the papers. I wouldn't be surprised if he weren't cooking something up as we speak.

June 20th, Thursday

*E*STHER *Rantzen has worked wonders over the last 22 years.* People forget what Esther has done for Britain. If it wasn't for Esther and her pioneering ways those dogs who sing would never have got any television coverage.

June 21st, Friday

ALAN *Titchmarsh – often imitated but never bettered.*

June 22nd, Saturday

*I*T *was a year ago I remember waking from a vivid dream.* It had all seemed so real. I was in a field completely naked along with Richard and Judy who were also completely nude. The three of us were skipping and jumping quite merrily and catching butterflies in a completely innocent fashion and I was really enjoying this dream until my excitement was dampened when a naked Fred Talbot cavorted on to the scene.

June 23rd, Sunday

A LOVELY *bunch a lads!* I find the AA service invaluable. If you're going on a long journey do what I do – give them a ring first and tell them where you're going and keep stopping on the way to let them know you're OK. I think it puts their minds at rest and avoids unnecessary worry.

June 24th, Monday

*M*Y *friend Lily has long been fascinated by frozen food.* Each to his or her own. I'm a tinned fruit fan myself, always have been, always will be.

A fruity treat for Mr Merton!

June 25th, Tuesday

'*T*HE *Nun's Story' is a film you can see again and
again.* It's a marvellous story with Audrey Hepburn
playing a nun called Sister Luke who goes to work in a
hospital in the Congo, as assistant to Dr Fortunati. And
of course she finds herself falling for Dr Fortunati as
there's not much else to look at in the Congo. But he's
an atheist you see, he doesn't know about God, and
what with her being a nun it's all very exciting. They
don't make them like that any more. Come on Quentin
Tarantino, shape yourself.

June 26th, Wednesday

*J*EFF *Banks – yes thanks! We could do with more
like him.*

June 27th, Thursday

*N*o *one out-wits Miss Marple. She's the sleuthing
spinster – a bit like Hercule Poirot with a handbag
and more of a tache.*

June 28th, Friday

*M*R *Merton – I love you.*

June 29th, Saturday
The Change

*I*T *can strike at any time – I remember a few years ago
we'd booked a fortnight in Southport, I kept thinking I
was so looking forward to it, what if I got a touch of the*

Menopause whilst on holiday. I went to the Doctor's and asked him to induce it, but he said they haven't got the technology. Something there for the NHS to think about.

June 30th, Sunday
HALF way through the year. Chin up.

 July

July 1st, Monday

A SUMMER'S SCENE
A special season Summer is!
The Summer sights and Summer sounds
The Summer smells
Summer tastes as well
And the Sunshine – It abounds!

July 2nd, Tuesday

*G*RACIE *Fields, so obviously an icon to young girl singers – many try to emulate her but without success! Look no further than Tina Turner.*

July 3rd, Wednesday

Our Wedding Anniversary

*A*s one of our wedding presents 38 years ago we received an up-to-the-minute Pyrex casserole dish with a see-through lid. The casserole dish has weathered the ups and downs of our marriage – in and out of the oven in both good and bad times. Like our marriage it's still going strong – holding in the meat and veg despite its age. How many modern marriages can boast that?

July 4th, Thursday, American Independence Day

DON'T be afraid of Americans! They're really just like us except more accustomed to crime.

July 5th, Friday

Curiosity and the Cat!

*M*Y *neighbours – the Hendersons (Cathy and Colin) – went on holiday to Greece for a fortnight.* They left me their keys in order to feed their cat, Henry. Isn't it funny how naturally curious the human race is. One day I found myself in their bedroom going through an old pile of love letters they'd hidden in the bottom of a drawer. I must say I was shocked at the lewd nature of some of the comments Colin had made. This is not the type of thing that should be written down for anyone to see. A friend of mine Lily was thoroughly disgusted when I showed her too.

July 6th, Saturday

NEVER underestimate Rolf Harris! He's a perennial.

July 7th, Sunday

*I*N *my day the sex word was taboo.* Nowadays you hear the word mentioned on TV and radio constantly. Especially on Channel 4 (Channel 4-letter words I call it). The word Penis was used 8 times on a programme presented by Margi Clarke. That's too many penises for anyone to handle, even Liverpudlian Margi Clarke!

July 8th, Monday

NATURE is a marvellous invention.

July 9th, Tuesday

*A*s an upstanding member of society I was recently called upon to attend Jury Service. It opened my eyes to the terrible waste of public money by the legal system. The trial lasted 7 days of which the last 6 were a waste of time as I had made my mind up within minutes of seeing the accused. His eyebrows were too close together and he had a look of the Cockney about him. I knew immediately that he was guilty.

We then had to sit through countless hours of stories proclaiming his innocence, although there was no way I was being swayed, even though the other 11 members of the jury disagreed. It is clear that they should be more selective in choosing jurors. This would surely help speed things along.

July 10th, Wednesday

> *AN ENGLISH GARDEN IN SUMMER*
> *Mowing the lawn! It's dad*
> *The kids await the ice-cream van*
> *What to do for tea's the thing?*
> *Have a salad! That's the plan!*

July 11th, Thursday

TREAT gas with respect. It's not a toy.

July 12th, Friday

*H*APPY *Birthday Molly Fallon.* Not everyone knows who you are but surely everyone can share the sentiment nevertheless.

July 13th, Saturday

*O*N *our annual trip to Southport, my friend and I, Lily, were blessed with a glorious sunny day which we spent sunbathing.* Finding myself stricken with chapped lips I helped myself to some Vaseline I came across in Lily's bag. I later confessed to Lily and told her that rubbing in the Vaseline had a marvellous effect on my chapped lips. It has the same effect on my piles she replied, much to my dismay. Always look before you leap! Especially where Vaseline is concerned.

July 14th, Sunday
Chalk and Cheese
EMILY Bishop and Erasure.

July 15th, Monday
A FRIEND *of mine Joan Deacon swore if she ever won the pools it would not change her life one iota.* Earlier this year she won £200,000 on the pools and immediately moved to Lytham St Anne's. What a liar! It's not the winning, it's the barefaced hypocrisy that upsets me.

July 16th, Tuesday
K ENDAL *mint cake is not cake at all, it's just sugar with a minty taste! How anyone could try to pretend it's a cake is beyond me.*

July 17th, Wednesday
KEN Russell film maker – genius or barmpot?

July 18th, Thursday
A Day Out
' *L* ET'S *have a run out,' I said to Mr Merton one bank holiday.* We decided upon the bustling town of Bakewell, famous of course for its novelty tarts. I packed a thermos flask and two rounds of sandwiches

Summer madness!

(corned beef) and we set off. All went according to plan until we got to Marple. The next thing we knew our Morris Minor car had ground to a halt on a country road. Neither of us being mechanically minded, we decided to ring the AA. Naturally, as we were running short of time to get to Bakewell, I told the AA I was a woman on my own in order to speed their arrival. Mr Merton happily agreed to hide behind a nearby tree upon the arrival of the friendly AA man. However, unbeknown to us, the damage was worse than we expected. Poor Mr Merton was left hiding behind the tree as the Morris Minor was towed away. I, of course, had to carry on the deceit and had to offer half the sandwiches to the AA man as part of the elaborate cover-up. It was midnight before a bedraggled Mr Merton returned home vowing never again to engage in subversive activities on the way to Bakewell.

July 19th, Friday
NEVER write off Mickey Rooney. Do so at your peril!

July 20th, Saturday
SQUEAKY shoes can be a burden! Keep them well polished and they'll not squeak as much. If they do persist, at least they'll look presentable.

July 21st, Sunday
ON a coach trip to the Blue John Mines (Derbyshire) I was seated next to my friend Mary Murray, who is

a lovely lady with a withered hand. I barely notice this
affliction and would never dream of drawing attention
to it. However, after a dispute between myself and Mary
Murray regarding the coach driver's age, I was shocked
to find myself pointing out her withered deformity to the
other unsuspecting passengers on the coach, and doing
impressions of her with my fingerless glove. Even the
kindest of souls can turn when backed into a corner.

July 22nd, Monday
DAVE Lee Travis – our thoughts are always with you.

July 23rd, Tuesday
A FRIEND *of mine Gwen Sharples is a dinner lady
at the local boys' primary school.* Early last year
she took it upon herself to serve larger portions to
the thinner boys and lesser portions to those of a
plumper stature, as a little experiment. However, her
tampering with nature was cut short due to unexpected
redundancies. The repercussions of her actions will
sadly never be known.

July 24th, Wednesday
WOMEN are different!

July 25th, Thursday
A FRIEND *of mine Jimi Hendrix (who shares his
name with a legendary rock guitarist) worked part
time for the Post Office (full time at Christmas).* If

on occasion he found his postman's sack a little too heavy he simply delivered the ones he felt were strictly necessary. He was a great comfort to pensioners as he refused to deliver bad news or astronomical bills. However, the Post Office took an unreasonable view of Jimi's local service. Jimi now spends his time sewing mailbags at Risley Remand. His life has come full circle! What a cruel knife Fate has twisted in Jimi's back.

July 26th, Friday
Malcolm's Birthday

*T*ODAY *is my son Malcolm's 35th birthday.* He seemingly never tells his friends that it's his birthday as no cards whatsoever arrive for him. He spends his birthday evening locked in his little bedroom which hasn't changed one iota since he was a boy. Occasionally I stand by the door and listen to the sounds of gentle sobbing. Happy birthday Malcolm. Happy Birthday son.

July 27th, Saturday

*F*ULL *marks to Paul Nicholas. He goes from strength to strength.*

July 28th, Sunday

*S*OME *time ago my son Malcolm developed a 'crush' on his dentist's assistant, a young red-haired girl called Linda Potter.* Try as he might he could not pluck up enough courage to ask her out on a date. He was

besotted by Linda Potter's freckles and lily-white skin.
For weeks he sought her company – inventing ailments
of a fictitious nature. After having had all his back
teeth capped and numerous fillings, I felt the need to
intervene and made myself an appointment for a check-
up. It turned out that Linda Potter had no designs on
my Malcolm and found his excessive dental work a put-
off. What was a loving mother to do in this situation?
The pain of motherhood is never-ending! Later that
evening I sat Malcolm down and explained to him
carefully how Linda Potter had earlier that day been
horrifically killed in a freak shipping disaster. A little
white lie perhaps, but sometimes you have to be cruel
to be kind. I managed to spare him this heartbreak, but
it saddens me to think I might not always be there for
him in the future.

July 29th, Monday

LYNDA *Carter really was a Wonder Woman.*

July 30th, Tuesday

*W*ELL *done Cilla Black.* She's managed to turn
all her negative points into positive ones. She
deserves every bit of her money-spinning success.

July 31st, Wednesday

THREE *cheers for the British Bobby!*

August

August 1st, Thursday

A FRIEND *of mine Ernest Hudson insists on always using the 24-hour clock system.* This is all very well if everyone takes part – but Ernest doesn't seem to realise people have other things to do.

August 2nd, Friday

F OREIGN *holidays are all well and good but to my mind Southport takes the biscuit!* It's got the whole kit and caboodle all within walking distance of the coach station.

August 3rd, Saturday

PERHAPS today is your birthday! Happy Birthday.

August 4th, Sunday

> ***DON'T FORGET YELLOW!***
> *Yellow, the colour of sunshine*
> *Yellow the colour of gold*
> *Yellow the colour of pilau rice*
> *Yes, yellow's a colour so bold!*

August 5th, Monday

*T*HE *Body Shop pride themselves on not testing their products on animals.* But what if some did fall on a dog? Something there for them to think about.

August 6th, Tuesday

A GOOD *idea for women on the Menopause.* Why not give them little stickers for the car so that they can park on double yellow lines?

August 7th, Wednesday

*T*ERRY *Christian is nobody's fool.* Once he finds his niche, watch him go.

August 8th, Thursday

*A*N *old friend of Mr Merton's, Patrick Gerard, has recently entered his second childhood.* Despite being 86 he is often to be found with a gang of youths, making a nuisance of himself in the precinct, spitting over the balcony at unsuspecting passers-by. Mr Merton was obviously concerned about his old friend and decided to have a quiet word with him. He thought he'd sorted the matter out once and for all, but as he turned to walk away he felt a blob of spittle hit the back of his neck and heard a loud raspberry. It is so sad that this man who fought so bravely in Burma is now a menace to society.

AUGUST

August 9th, Friday

FINGERS crossed for the Ozone layer. A premature Ice Age is the last thing we need in the North West.

August 10th, Saturday

*L*IFE *is never so bad after a cup of tea.* When we are troubled in any way, we British put the kettle on and make a cup of char. Tea is the comforter in a crisis. When I got a phone call saying Mr Merton had just fallen off a ladder in the next street, my first instinct was of course to reach for the kettle. After a soothing cup of tea I rushed round without delay to find him laying there in agony. Life's tragedies come and go dear readers, tea is constant.

August 11th, Sunday

'*W*HY *go out for a burger when you've got steak at home,' says Paul Newman about his lovely wife Nanette, and he should know.*

August 12th, Monday

A LEARNED *keyhole surgery pioneer friend of mine Professor Alastair McQuitty employs a daily cleaner, as his job means many long hours at the hospital at the cutting edge of Neurosurgery.* It's such a shame he will never know the satisfaction of looking at a freshly scrubbed step, a polished china cabinet

Everyone's entitled to a piece of Nature – it's
not stealing!

or a spotless oven. None of us fully appreciate the sacrifices neurosurgeons have to make.

August 13th, Tuesday

*R*ICHARD *Stilgoe has never gone off the boil. Who* can forget those hilarious and irreverent songs at the piano?

August 14th, Wednesday

A FRIEND *of mine Nellie, a lovely lady who has never quite come to terms with the death of Cary Grant, is fanatical about competitions.* She has so far won a set of heated rollers, a holiday for two at Eurodisney and a year's supply of table salt. Obsessive as she is, she refuses to enter the National Lottery, dismissing it as purely for amateurs. Wise up Nellie, a flutter is a flutter.

August 15th, Thursday

*I*F *only Nigel Kennedy teamed up with Aled Jones then we'd really see something.*

August 16th, Friday

A FRIEND *of mine Norma Cowles started The Change at Pontins in Torquay but there were absolutely no Menopausal facilities there whatsoever. Something there for Judith Chalmers to think about.*

August 17th, Saturday
Elvis Remembered
*E*VERY *year on the anniversary of Elvis's death we are bombarded with Elvis films on TV and Elvis records on the radio all day.* How can we be assured the same thing won't happen when Michael Ball dies?

August 18th, Sunday
*A*s *far as the Government is concerned the Menopause is being pushed aside in favour of Maastricht.*

August 19th, Monday
*W*ELL *done Anthony Hopkins.* He's single-handedly made being Welsh popular again.

August 20th, Tuesday
*I*T *is exactly a year ago since I met Richard and Judy on 'This Morning'.* It was such a privilege to see what they are really like behind the façade. I'm sure they won't mind me telling you, a happier more in-love couple you couldn't meet, and considering the vast age difference this surely is an achievement. I was reminded of the old adage 'Love Conquers All' and I got to meet Fred Talbot as well. Oh happy day!

August 21st, Wednesday

*H*ELLO *all you Bantam-weight boxers!* Here's a story for you. On a wrong number my son Malcolm inadvertently got through to Barry McGuigan the little bantam-weight boxer from Ireland. Despite his busy schedule he happily spent ten minutes chatting away willy-nilly to this once famous boxer.

August 22nd, Thursday

*T*o *be a pop star in the popular parade you need a gimmick.* Alvin Stardust had a leather glove, Morrissey had daffodils, Liberace liked his rings and Midge Ure – his gimmick was being very small. A gimmick can really pay off. Remember the more outlandish the better.

August 23rd, Friday

*D*ieting *can be hazardous!* Take Oprah Winfrey, you never quite know where you are with her. I was fiddling with the horizontal hold for ages one week till I realised she'd put on 3 stones since the week before.

August 24th, Saturday

*O*n *a recent trip to the abattoirs, my friend Lily remarked on what a wonderful sacrifice animals make on our behalf.*

August 25th, Sunday

*M*r *Merton was as shocked as I was to find my son Malcolm had hidden Adult magazines under his bed.* So sensitive he was to Malcolm's feelings we agreed never to mention it and Mr Merton thoughtfully confiscated them and secured them in his garden shed. He was in there confiscating them for hours. Apparently they were very similar to some he'd come across as a youth.

August 26th, Monday

*F*ull *marks to Björk!* I think there should be far more Eskimos in the popular parade. Björk is an inspiration! Back in Iceland she used to sit crosslegged outside her igloo singing haunting melodies. On hearing her voice fish used to jump up out of the ice and she would catch them in her mouth. One day a record producer who was skating by heard her and the rest is history. Apparently when she came over here they told her to drop the fish-eating side of her act as it wasn't working.

August 27th, Tuesday

I WAS at my friend Doris Clarke's house one day. She's not the most attractive of ladies, she's got a look of Judge Pickles about her. We were talking about how Father Time ravishes your looks and her husband Bill put down his *People's Friend* and said, 'Doris, you'll always be beautiful to me.' The effect would have been greater if he had not been partially sighted in his good eye, but the thought was there and it perked Doris up. The next day she was plucking her whiskers from her chin like there was no tomorrow.

August 28th, Wednesday

R INGO Starr never thought he could top his rock and roll lifestyle with the world-famous Beatles. But now he's starting all over again, voicing Thomas the Tank Engine videos.

August 29th, Thursday

C OME on Hollywood moguls! Let's have a remake of 'Beauty and the Beast' with Rula Lenska and Dennis Waterman.

August 30th, Friday

I REMEMBER *my first kiss.* He was an American GI.
It was during the war when Americans were very
popular. He kissed me full on the lips and I remember
feeling very different afterwards, he had left his chewing
gum in my mouth. There was still a bit of flavour left
as I recall so I made the most of it. Times were hard.

August 31st, Saturday

BEATRIX *Potter has simply lost touch with the youth
of today.*

September

September 1st, Sunday

*D*AVID *Frost is most famous for his in-depth intellectual interviews with world statesmen, but he has really come into his own presenting 'Through the Keyhole' where we get to have a look at the homes of famous celebrities. Well done David! You got there in the end.*

September 2nd, Monday

*W*HAT *an apt name – Johnny Rotten. In my opinion he was.*

September 3rd, Tuesday

I COULD *never be a feminist/lesbian as there is nothing more pleasurable to me than the sight of the bottom of the washing basket on a wash day.*

September 4th, Wednesday

'*I*'M *Spartacus, I'm Spartacus.' How these words fill me with emotion every time I remember the moving scene from the epic film, the name of which escapes me for the moment.*

September 5th, Thursday

How long will it be before everyone realises James Galway is not a flash in the pan.

September 6th, Friday

Menopause is the Great Leveller

*P*EOPLE *think the Menopause goes unnoticed.* I can tell even with celebrities with all their money who is on the change. Gloria Hunniford on a recent edition of *Pebble Mill* had Menopause written all over her.

September 7th, Saturday

*I*F ONLY *Cleo Laine could have been bothered to have learned the words to her songs, she'd have surely become more popular with the general public.*

September 8th, Sunday

A FRIEND *of Arthur Capstick, cherub faced David Gorman, insists on walking around at all times of the day with very little covering.* Even on the coldest winter mornings he is to be found wearing nothing but a string vest, studded boots and a Magnum PI type moustache. I suggested to Arthur that he needs discipline and Arthur readily agreed.

September 9th, Monday

*E*VERYONE *is unique, apart from a friend of mine, Josephine Curly, and she would be the first to admit it.*

September 10th, Tuesday

> **GOOD OLD-FASHIONED AUTUMN (NOT FALL)**
> *A season the Americans call*
> *Not Autumn but 'Fall'*
> *Is Autumn.*
> *Names like these, the Yanks like to shorten!*
> *We call it Autumn, if you please;*
> *'Fall' is what the leaves do, from the trees.*

September 11th, Wednesday
Chalk and Cheese
Tokyo and Macclesfield.

September 12th, Thursday

ROGER Cook, he's such a bruiser!

September 13th, Friday

How disappointed Malcolm was when spiteful children at school revealed to him that animals do not talk and that it was Johnny Morris all along.

September 14th, Saturday, Jewish New Year

HAPPY New Year to Jewish folk.

September 15th, Sunday

Although to look at me now you would never guess, as a young girl I was renowned locally for my slim figure and understated beauty, and was often compared to Julia Roberts.

September 16th, Monday

A POEM FOR MR MERTON

*If I could pick someone at random
It would be you to ride on my tandem (of life).*

September 17th, Tuesday

ANNABEL Giles – a true delight.

September 18th, Wednesday

Emmerdale has done much to advertise the countryside. So many town folk have sold up and moved out into the country, trying to emulate this idyllic existence. What people don't realise, however, is that this is a fool's errand. *Emmerdale* is merely a TV soap opera and disguises much of the realities of country life, such as unsightly cow dung hidden behind purposely placed extras.

September 19th, Thursday

*E*URO-DISNEY *was always doomed to failure!* How they could possibly expect little children to understand Mickey Mouse speaking French is beyond me.

September 20th, Friday

How easy it is to teach children nowadays with the wealth of early-learning toys available instead of having to make do with two clothes pegs, an elastic band and an old shoe box.

September 21st, Saturday

WHY not take time out to reflect on the success of the multi-talented Sean Maguire.

September 22nd, Sunday

I THINK that a lot of my son Malcolm's problems stem from the fact that at his primary school there was a boy in his class called Malcolm Morton and the two Malcolms were always getting confused. My Malcolm could never quite come to terms with this and I believe the scars of this traumatic childhood dilemma have never been truly healed.

Girl about town!

September 23rd, Monday

*I*T'S *well over a year since Hugh Grant was arrested for lewd conduct with a prostitute. Isn't it high time we forgot all about it!*

September 24th, Tuesday

*F*OR *no reason at all this is my favourite day. Why don't you have a favourite day of your own. There's plenty to choose from.*

September 25th, Wednesday

*R*EMEMBER *there's only one of you but there's simply millions of other people.*

September 26th, Thursday

*T*HE *Americans love little Dudley Moore and have clasped him to their breasts whilst managing to fob us off with Loyd Grossman.*

September 27th, Friday

I CAN'T *help feeling that Mickey Dolenz of 'The Monkees' fame was clearly misunderstood for many years. Only time will tell.*

September 28th, Saturday

*T*ODAY *let's everyone pull together and aim for world peace. Even if it's just for one day it will have been worth it.*

September 29th, Sunday

A NEIGHBOUR *of mine Pearl Myers (née Goffin) has never once left the confines of Heaton Norris.* She has never been lured by strange-sounding exotic places like Belgium or Dundee (famous for its cake). She has managed to lead an exciting life, but has kept it local.

September 30th, Monday

LET'S all get behind Chris Evans – it's so good to see a ginger-haired person doing well.

October

October 1st, Tuesday

A FRIEND *of mine, Freda Blonden, has fifteen cats and would be the first to admit that there is always a distinct aroma of cat urine about her person.* Whilst being a feline's greatest friend, me and my friend Lily simply can't abide the stench. It is a shame because we used to be really friendly with her and now Lily and I find ourselves writing anonymous letters about her to the local papers.

October 2nd, Wednesday

LILAC FOREVER
Lilac is the colour for me,
Lilac is the tops.
Lilac is the colour, you see,
That pulls out all the stops.

October 3rd, Thursday

*C*ORNED *beef is no longer a poor person's food!* Apparently it is now being served in London's top restaurants as a delicacy, according to my friend Rene Fletcher. However, you do have to request it specifically and be prepared to stick to your guns.

October 4th, Friday

THERE is no age limit on Gary Lineker! He is a treat for young and old alike.

October 5th, Saturday

*M*ALCOLM *was never the most athletic of boys and suffered from problems with balance when under competition.* School sports days were always a traumatic occasion for me, watching Malcolm trying to put a little brave face on coming last in every event. So distraught I became one year, I Blue Tacked his egg to his spoon for the egg-and-spoon race. However, when this was discovered at the end of the race, I found myself with no option but to blame Malcolm and vigorously slapped the back of his legs for all to see.

Although Malcolm's triumph was short lived at least I gave him the opportunity of tasting the glory of victory for what has turned out to be the only time in his life. What more could a mother do?

October 6th, Sunday

THE Queen has forsaken fashion for comfort. Nowhere is this more obvious than in her choice of clothes and husband.

October 7th, Monday

BOB Monkhouse is a natural.

October 8th, Tuesday

SPARE a thought for the wives of imprisoned criminals who aren't lucky enough to have their own TV series like Pauline and Linda from 'Birds of a Feather'.

October 9th, Wednesday, Columbus Day

HE'S done very well for himself, Christopher Columbus! He lost out on America being named after him but they've more than made it up to him with his own day. Happy Columbus Day.

October 10th, Thursday

MONEY can't buy happiness but, as my friend Lily points out, it can certainly buy alcohol.

Top gear!

October 11th, Friday

I'VE often thought Mr Merton would make a marvellous after-dinner speaker. He has a way of embroidering and embellishing the most minute details into his conversation that, although not strictly true, adds entertainment value to what would otherwise be a meaningless story.

October 12th, Saturday

KATIE Puckrik – what's she all about?

October 13th, Sunday

GEOFF Lloyd, our local apprentice butcher, is famed throughout the district for his unique ability to differentiate between different types of cheese purely by taste. He is often to be seen demonstrating his singular talent in the local pub to an interested yet disbelieving crowd. Where he got his talent we will never know, as both his parents confess to being totally indifferent to dairy produce.

October 14th, Monday

DANNY Baker is not a fat balding irritating cockney know-all and I won't have anyone say he is.

October 15th, Tuesday

EVERYONE loves the smell of lavender! It knocks the spots off fancy foreign perfumes.

October 16th, Wednesday

*W*E *all know the feeling when you're sworn to keep a secret and you find yourself divulging the details to a large group of friends.* Remember, it is not your fault if they then pass this secret on and it gets back to the original teller. This is simply nature taking its course.

October 17th, Thursday

*W*HAT *have Henry Fonda and Jane Fonda got in common? They are both part of the same famous Fonda acting family, the Fondas.*

October 18th, Friday

I RECENTLY *had to phone the doctor, being a little worried that Malcolm had got a night cold as I kept finding used tissues beside his bed.* During the daytime not a sniffle! For some reason the doctor wanted to see Malcolm on his own and seemed unduly concerned about his eyesight.

October 19th, Saturday

*D*AME *Fortune has recently smiled on popular songsmith Shaun Ryder, giving him a brand new lease of life! Great things are expected in 1996 Shaun!*

October 20th, Sunday

*W*HEN *I was learning to drive, my instructor, Ken Niblock from Niblock Driving School (it's his own* *company), instructed me to drive with my hands in the ten-to-two position on the steering wheel.* However, I found this to be a bit too early and prefer the twenty-to-three position. In the new twenty-four-hour clock system, currently popular, this becomes fourteen forty.

October 21st, Monday

*H*AS *there ever been a better TV programme made than 'Casualty'?* Yes! 'Heartbeat', with young Nick Berry, where he plays a fresh-faced police constable. It wins hands down.

October 22nd, Tuesday

*O*N *my wedding day I purposely arrived half an hour late to ensure Mr Merton was not just marrying me on a whim but had serious intentions.* When I eventually arrived I found Mr Merton had entered into a game of Cribbage with the priest and two ushers, and I had to have the wedding car circle the church until the game had finished. Although Mr Merton had lost all our honeymoon money I couldn't say anything as it was his entrepreneurial spirit that had attracted me in the first place.

October 23rd, Wednesday

I'M *still in two minds about unilateral disarmament.* On one hand I think I know what it means, on the other hand I'm clueless.

October 24th, Thursday
My heart goes out to Dolph Lundgren.

October 25th, Friday
In the song 'Tie a Yellow Ribbon' we are all very pleased at the end when there are 100 yellow ribbons tied around the old oak tree. But let us not forget that the man in the song must have done something wrong to have been imprisoned in the first place. Crime is wrong no matter how much American singers try to disguise it with fancy lyrics.

October 26th, Saturday
Well done the inventor of bay windows! It's the nearest you can get to all round vision in the comfort of your own home.

October 27th, Sunday
I remember the time when you could never get enough of Yoko Ono. How things change.

October 28th, Monday
You may think, dear reader, that there are only three members of my family: myself, Mr Merton and Malcolm Merton. There are in fact five, including my two dogs Mitzy and Sadie, who contribute much to our family life in their own way. I try not to have a favourite and to divide my attention equally but, I must confess, at times it is easier with the two dogs who are often less demanding and do not sulk as much.

October 29th, Tuesday

A FRIEND *of mine, Mary Chadwick, refuses to move with the times.* She is making a rod for her own back. Try telling her that though!

October 30th, Wednesday

EVERYONE is beautiful in their own way, so says the popular song. I assume this excludes Diane Conlan and her gargoyle-like features.

October 31st, Thursday, Hallowe'en

MELVIN Bragg – can anyone make head or tail of him?

November 1st, Friday
*D*UST *will always find its way into those unseen nooks and crannies!* Forget it. If it's there, it can't be settling on the china cabinet. That's scientific fact.

November 2nd, Saturday
*O*NE *morning I was passing my son Malcolm his Branflakes when I noticed red blotches on one side of his neck.* Knowing about these so called 'love bites' perpetrated by modern society I enquired tactfully if there was a young lady in his life that he hadn't told me and his father about. He was quick to deny any such involvement which made me suspicious. Pressing him further he broke down and admitted that what I'd mistaken for love bites were in fact the latest in a spate of boils he had been endeavouring to lance himself in his boxroom, without medical supervision. Poor Malcolm, he had only just conquered his impetigo. It never rains but it pours!

November 3rd, Sunday
*G*ET *familiar with plums and other fruit.*

101

November 4th, Monday

*A*RTIFICIAL *Insemination used to be just for animals, not any more!* Young barren couples can now take themselves off to London and come back fully impregnated. Animals can still teach us a thing or two!

November 5th, Tuesday

> *A CAUTIONARY VERSE FOR BONFIRE NIGHT*
> *Bonfire Night!*
> *Such a delight!*
> *See the children squeal with glee*
> *The Catherine wheel's stuck up a tree.*
> *'I'll rescue it,' brave Daddy says,*
> *Next thing you know, he's all ablaze.*
> *What a bother, what a fuss,*
> *Never do what Daddy does.*

November 6th, Wednesday

I HAVE *noticed the Daily Star are more imaginative with their bikini-clad models.* They at least try to make them fit in with the news. If it's bonfire night they might be holding a sparkler. If it's Christmas one'll have Santa's hat on.

November 7th, Thursday

I RECENTLY *spent an entire afternoon listening to my friend Beattie Gosworth boasting of her son's (Gordon Gosworth) achievements as a salesman for security windows.* She regaled me with tales of her son's company car and expense account. By the time she'd finished I found myself wishing my son Malcolm was more of an achiever like Gordon. I returned home weary with the injustice of it all. As I entered the front room I found Malcolm sponge painting on the kitchen table, happy as a sandboy. We can only love our children for what they are. Not all our sons can be Gordon Gosworths.

November 8th, Friday

*E*VERYONE *has a novel inside them.* Jeffrey Archer has never been afraid to get it out, usually to please his female fans.

November 9th, Saturday

A FRIEND *of Mr Merton's, Tommy Tatlock, has what*

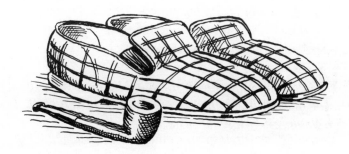

I call a very lavatorial sense of humour. My friend Lily however finds him hilarious. How I loathe to hear them both guffawing uproariously at Tommy's toiletry innuendo. Surely this is Nature after all and is not to be mocked out of hand.

November 10th, Sunday

WHATEVER you say about David Mellor – love or loathe him – you've got to admire his spunk!

November 11th, Monday

*A*s a young man, Mr Merton was enamoured by *Gina Lollobrigida.* Seeing her recently on TV he remarked that age and the ravages of time had in no way withered her beauty. I had to point out that we were, of course, watching a film that had been made in 1957 when she was still a girl. At this Mr Merton became quite unreasonable and refused to discuss it.

November 12th, Tuesday

WENDY Richards is a feast for the eyes.

November 13th, Wednesday

*W*HEN *asked the secret of his success local entrepreneur Richard Michael stated that he never discusses business ever. It is this secrecy that is the hallmark of his success.*

November 14th, Thursday
My Friend Lily's Birthday

I NEVER forget this date, as she never lets me. Lily leaves the Argos catalogue opened for weeks with some fancy item circled in the hope I'll see it. Lily shares her birthday with Elizabeth Taylor, God bless her. However, that's where the similarity ends.

November 15th, Friday

In the midst of life we are in death the old saying goes, but the reverse is also true!

November 16th, Saturday
Chalk and Cheese

Liza Minnelli and Cliff Michelmore.

November 17th, Sunday

In the olden days when we had to use newspaper for toilet paper, Mr Merton would become so engrossed in a news story he would temporarily forget his mission. With the advent of soft toilet paper Mr Merton is much quicker about his ablutions but now less informed current affairs-wise. Progress really is swings and roundabouts.

November 18th, Monday

Stopping in a hotel one time I elected for the Continental Breakfast only to find it was nothing but fancy bread and jam under another guise. These

At the helm!

hoteliers have been pulling the wool over our eyes for too long.

November 19th, Tuesday
SHIRLEY Temple has surely lost it in recent years. Her decision to abandon her little-girl look has cost her dearly.

November 20th, Wednesday
SCIENCE fiction, involving visions of the future, is totally unnecessary and a waste of people's energy. If we could only be patient it'd all reveal itself in the fullness of time without the need for Steven Spielberg and the like.

November 21st, Thursday
BERYL Carpenter is one of those people who won't say a bad word about anyone no matter how much my friend Lily and I try to goad her or trick her into it. Poor Beryl, she doesn't seem to realise the good-natured fun you can have at other people's expense behind their backs.

November 22nd, Friday
TORVILL and Dean have got it on the ice! But off the ice you've got to hand it to Richard and Judy! The best off-ice team in the world!

November 23rd, Saturday

B<small>RAVO</small> *Betty Ford, allowing your name to be associated with drunkards and ne'er-do-wells despite your connections with the US president.*

November 24th, Sunday

V<small>IV</small> *Nicholson and her phrase 'I'm going to spend, spend, spend' was emblazoned on the front pages of every newspaper in the country.* But would the media have been so interested in her had she not won a fortune on the Pools. I doubt it very much and so does my friend Lily.

November 25th, Monday

O<small>H</small> *how I'd love to see the invitations sent for a Henry Fonda fondu party.*

November 26th, Tuesday

N<small>OT</small> *all paranormal phenomena happen in the United States.* Recently my friend Betty changed her shoe size almost overnight from 5 to 4½ without any logical explanation whatsoever. Betty's claims have never been proven, however, as her husband is entirely disinterested in the whole affair and refuses to allow her to pursue the matter with the correct authorities.

November 27th, Wednesday

A STRANGER *is only a friend you haven't met, I constantly tell my son Malcolm to encourage him to remain optimistic. His potential for friendship is huge.*

November 28th, Thursday, Thanksgiving Day (USA)

*T*HE *Americans never thought to elect themselves a patron saint but they've come up with the next best thing. Happy Thanksgiving.*

November 29th, Friday

A FRIEND *of mine Norma Cowels often says that she has never been well since she moved to Peterborough.* However, she will not concede that she was eight at the time of the move and is now seventy-four.

November 30th, Saturday, Saint Andrew's Day

*W*HEREVER *you are, whatever you're doing, this day is Saint Andrew's Day. Happy Saint Andrew's Day to you.*

December

December 1st, Sunday

Angry Winter Poem
Winter is cold
When you are getting old
and the long nights unfold
Authorities be told!

December 2nd, Monday

Modern radiators are a boon but do they foster untold diseases? We may never know!

December 3rd, Tuesday

All the big stores are filled with expensive toys and computer games at this time of year. It makes me think back to when my Malcolm was young. Whatever we bought him he still had the most fun with an empty Bacofoil roll and his little pet hamster.

December 4th, Wednesday

'University Challenge' is all well and good but not everybody has been to university. Everyone has used a catchphrase though and Roy Walker has done well to capitalise on this.

December 5th, Thursday

*A*N *able-bodied friend of mine Molly Potts is incensed by pornography.* If anything of a lewd, rude or explicit nature comes on TV she rings me up immediately to inform me which channel it's on. If I'm not in it's OK because I can rest assured she will have videoed it for us to watch at a later date. Molly is ever vigilant in her fight against pornography.

December 6th, Friday

*O*NE *night Malcolm asked what it would be like to be kissed by a woman. He seems less and less interested in sponge painting these days.*

December 7th, Saturday

*K*ATE *Adie could be a bit of a looker if only she made more of an effort.* On some of these location shots she looks as though make-up was the last thing on her mind.

December 8th, Sunday

*I*T *is ten years to the day Mr Merton had an unwanted cyst removed from under his arm. We often sit and imagine the size of it now had we just let it grow willy-nilly.*

December 9th, Monday

*T*ERRY *Wogan is so versatile; he can talk a load of old blarney on TV and on radio.*

December 10th, Tuesday

*M*Y *friend Lily and I are both big fans of singing sensation Kenny Rogers.* He is the one country and western legend to bridge that trans-Atlantic gap between Nashville, Tennessee, and Heaton Norris, Stockport.

December 11th, Wednesday

I HOPE *fame will never change me and that I'll always have space for Mr Merton and my son Malcolm in my busy schedule (time allowing).*

December 12th, Thursday

*T*HIS *is the day I usually set aside for taking all the net curtains down in my house for washing.* I always replace them as soon as possible as I feel

naked and exposed to the outside world without them. Also, I can't peep at goings-on in the street without being easily spotted.

December 13th, Friday
*J*OAN *Collins says you are what you eat.* She reached this conclusion following experiences in the swinging sixties and is very careful about what she puts in her mouth these days.

December 14th, Saturday
A YEAR *ago today Mr Merton issued an ultimatum: the dogs go or he does.*

December 15th, Sunday
A YEAR *ago today Mr Merton returned from his sister's with his tail between his legs.*

December 16th, Monday
*P*AVAROTTI *may well be the finest tenor the world has ever known.* Such a pity everybody's first impression of him is what a big fat man.

December 17th, Tuesday
*S*PAM *helped us win the war! How soon we forget.*

December 18th, Wednesday
*W*HENEVER *I'm in the company of Mr Merton's sister Anne, I can't help thinking what an embarrassing*

problem body odour is, but I would never risk hurting her feelings by mentioning it to her or to another living soul for that matter.

December 19th, Thursday

RADIO is a marvellous invention as it makes you feel like you're the only person that the DJ is talking to. Never is this more true than in the case of 'Signal Cheshire'.

December 20th, Friday

> *A YULETIDE RHYME FOR MR MERTON*
> *With your Mistletoe it's a kiss you seek*
> *You can have one – on the cheek.*

December 21st, Saturday

NOWADAYS the youth are obsessed with Gameboys and Martina Navratilova – in my day you made do with a couple of conkers and Billie Jean King.

December 22nd, Sunday

WITH Christmas decorations being so expensive why not do what I do, improvise. Last year I made a lovely baby Jesus out of old egg boxes and what I did was I used one of my old hair nets for a beard.

115

Festive fun!

December 23rd, Monday
A Mother's Pride

*H*ow I remember with pride the year Malcolm starred in the School nativity play. My heart was filled with joy at seeing Malcolm portray one of the shepherds. Malcolm played the quieter of the shepherds, the one who is bedazzled by the whole affair and doesn't seem to know what's going on.

December 24th, Tuesday, Christmas Eve

*O*NE *day I hope to write my own autobiography and share the trials and tribulations of life's ups and downs, and maybe time it just right for the Christmas market.*

December 25th, Wednesday, Christmas Day

A HAPPY Christmas to one and all. Why not invite an old person into your home this Christmas time. Spoil them with turkey and all the trimmings, and I think £14.50 is about right to charge them.

December 26th, Thursday, Boxing Day

*M*R *Merton's sister Anne always comes round on Boxing Day.* She mistakenly thinks she has the look of Bette Davis about her, as Bette appeared in the film 'All About Eve'. No matter how Mr Merton and I try, we cannot see the resemblance but she will not be told. She will not acknowledge that Bette Davis never had a hunchback. Mr Merton believes the resemblance to be nearer Charles Laughton.

December 27th, Friday

I'M *sorry, blubbered Malcolm, tears streaming down his little face, his head hung low in shame, as he showed me the broken pieces of a saucer he had been playing with.* I know objects are not important and can always be replaced, but I gave his legs a good slapping anyway. You could hit children in those days, right or wrong.

December 28th, Saturday

*O*NCE *upon a time smocks were worn by village idiots.* Nowadays they are sported by pregnant ladies without any regard for the history of this garment.

December 29th, Sunday

*W*ILL *people please stop telling Dave Bowie he can act.*

December 30th, Monday

*L*EARNING *to love yourself is the greatest love of all, says George Benson in the popular song.* I learned to love myself in the early eighties and have never looked back.

December 31st, Tuesday

*T*HIS *year has had its good times and its bad times, its tears and joy, but through it all there has remained one constant: 'Mrs Merton's Friendship Book', always there when you need a friend and reasonably priced when you average it out.*